IF FOUND, PLEASE
RETURN TO:

Name

Address

Phone number

Email

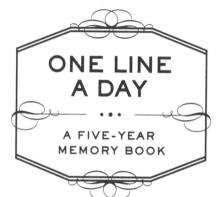

ONE LINE
A DAY

• • •

A FIVE-YEAR
MEMORY BOOK

CHRONICLE BOOKS

SAN FRANCISCO

ISBN 978-0-8118-7019-1

Manufactured in China
Design by Kristen Hewitt
Typeset in Sackers Gothic and Archer
Chronicle Books endeavors to use environmentally
responsible paper in its gift and stationery products.

30 29 28 27

Chronicle Books LLC
680 Second Street
San Francisco, CA 94107
www.chroniclebooks.com

A condensed, comparative
record for five years,
for recording events most
worthy of remembrance.

HOW TO USE THIS BOOK

To begin, turn to today's calendar date, and fill in
the year at the top of the page's first entry. Here,
you can add your thoughts on the present day's
events. On the next day, turn the page and fill in
the date accordingly. Do likewise throughout the
year. When the year has ended, start the next year
in the second entry space on the page, and so on
through the remaining years.

20......

20......

20......

20......

20......

20......

20......

20......

20......

20......

JANUARY 3

20......

20......

20......

20......

20......

JANUARY 4

20......

20......

20......

20......

20......

JANUARY 5

20......

20......

20......

20......

20......

JANUARY 6

20......

20......

20......

20......

20......

JANUARY 7

20......

20......

20......

20......

20......

20......

20......

20......

20......

20......

20......

20......

20......

20......

20......

JANUARY 10

20......

20......

20......

20......

20......

20......

20......

20......

20......

20......

JANUARY 12

20......

20......

20......

20......

20......

JANUARY 13

20......

20......

20......

20......

20......

JANUARY 14

20......

20......

20......

20......

20......

JANUARY 15

20......

20......

20......

20......

20......

JANUARY 16

20......

20......

20......

20......

20......

JANUARY 17

20......

20......

20......

20......

20......

JANUARY 18

20......

20......

20......

20......

20......

20......

20......

20......

20......

20......

20......

20......

20......

20......

20......

JANUARY 21

20......

20......

20......

20......

20......

JANUARY 22

20......

20......

20......

20......

20......

20......

20......

20......

20......

20......

JANUARY 24

20......

20......

20......

20......

20......

JANUARY 25

20......

20......

20......

20......

20......

20......

20......

20......

20......

20......

JANUARY 27

20......

20......

20......

20......

20......

JANUARY 28

20......

20......

20......

20......

20......

JANUARY 29

20......

20......

20......

20......

20......

20......

_____

20......

_____

20......

_____

20......

_____

20......

_____

JANUARY 31

20___

20___

20___

20___

20___

20......

20......

20......

20......

20......

FEBRUARY 2

20......

20......

20......

20......

20......

20......

20......

20......

20......

20......

FEBRUARY 4

20___

20___

20___

20___

20___

20......

20......

20......

20......

20......

FEBRUARY 6

20......

20......

20......

20......

20......

FEBRUARY 7

20___

20___

20___

20___

20___

FEBRUARY 8

20......

20......

20......

20......

20......

FEBRUARY 9

20......

20......

20......

20......

20......

FEBRUARY 10

20......

20......

20......

20......

20......

FEBRUARY 11

20......

20......

20......

20......

20......

FEBRUARY 12

20......

20......

20......

20......

20......

FEBRUARY 13

20......

20......

20......

20......

20......

20......

20......

20......

20......

20......

FEBRUARY 15

20......

20......

20......

20......

20......

FEBRUARY 16

20......

20......

20......

20......

20......

FEBRUARY 17

20......

_____

20......

_____

20......

_____

20......

_____

20......

_____

20......

20......

20......

20......

20......

FEBRUARY 19

20......

20......

20......

20......

20......

20......

20......

20......

20......

20......

20......

20......

20......

20......

20......

20......

20......

20......

20......

20......

20......

20......

20......

20......

20......

FEBRUARY 24

20......

20......

20......

20......

20......

FEBRUARY 25

20......

20......

20......

20......

20......

FEBRUARY 26

20......

20......

20......

20......

20......

FEBRUARY 27

20......

20......

20......

20......

20......

FEBRUARY 28

20......

20......

20......

20......

20......

FEBRUARY 29

20......

20......

20......

20......

20......

MARCH 1

20......

20......

20......

20......

20......

MARCH 2

20......

20......

20......

20......

20......

MARCH 3

20......

20......

20......

20......

20......

MARCH 4

20......

20......

20......

20......

20......

MARCH 5

20......

20......

20......

20......

20......

MARCH 6

20......

20......

20......

20......

20......

MARCH 7

20......

20......

20......

20......

20......

MARCH 8

20......

20......

20......

20......

20......

MARCH 9

20......

20......

20......

20......

20......

MARCH 10

20......

20......

20......

20......

20......

MARCH 11

20......

20......

20......

20......

20......

MARCH 12

20......

20......

20......

20......

20......

MARCH 13

20......

20......

20......

20......

20......

MARCH 14

20......

20......

20......

20......

20......

MARCH 15

20......

20......

20......

20......

20......

MARCH 16

20......

20......

20......

20......

20......

MARCH 17

20......

20......

20......

20......

20......

MARCH 18

20......

20......

20......

20......

20......

MARCH 19

20......

20......

20......

20......

20......

20......

20......

20......

20......

20......

MARCH 21

20......

20......

20......

20......

20......

20......

20......

20......

20......

20......

MARCH 23

20......

20......

20......

20......

20......

20......

20......

20......

20......

20......

MARCH 25

20......

20......

20......

20......

20......

MARCH 26

20......

20......

20......

20......

20......

20......

20......

20......

20......

20......

20......

20......

20......

20......

20......

MARCH 29

20......

20......

20......

20......

20......

20......

20......

20......

20......

20......

20......

20......

20......

20......

20......

20......

20......

20......

20......

20......

APRIL 2

20......

20......

20......

20......

20......

APRIL 3

20......

20......

20......

20......

20......

APRIL 4

20......

20......

20......

20......

20......

20......

20......

20......

20......

20......

APRIL 6

20......

20......

20......

20......

20......

20......

20......

20......

20......

20......

APRIL 8

20......

20......

20......

20......

20......

APRIL 9

20......

20......

20......

20......

20......

APRIL 10

20......

20......

20......

20......

20......

APRIL 11

20......

20......

20......

20......

20......

APRIL 12

20......

20......

20......

20......

20......

APRIL 13

20......

20......

20......

20......

20......

20......

20......

20......

20......

20......

APRIL 15

20......

20......

20......

20......

20......

20......

20......

20......

20......

20......

20......

20......

20......

20......

20......

APRIL 18

20......

20......

20......

20......

20......

APRIL 19

20......

20......

20......

20......

20......

APRIL 20

20......

20......

20......

20......

20......

APRIL 21

20......

20......

20......

20......

20......

20......

20......

20......

20......

20......

APRIL 23

20......

20......

20......

20......

20......

APRIL 24

20......

20......

20......

20......

20......

APRIL 25

20......

20......

20......

20......

20......

APRIL 26

20......

20......

20......

20......

20......

APRIL 27

20......

20......

20......

20......

20......

APRIL 28

20......

20......

20......

20......

20......

20......

20......

20......

20......

20......

APRIL 30

20......

20......

20......

20......

20......

MAY 1

20......

20......

20......

20......

20......

MAY 2

20......

20......

20......

20......

20......

MAY 3

20......

20......

20......

20......

20......

MAY 4

20......

20......

20......

20......

20......

MAY 5

20......

20......

20......

20......

20......

MAY 6

20......

20......

20......

20......

20......

MAY 7

20......

20......

20......

20......

20......

20......

20......

20......

20......

20......

MAY 9

20......

20......

20......

20......

20......

MAY 10

20......

20......

20......

20......

20......

MAY 11

20......

20......

20......

20......

20......

MAY 12

20......

20......

20......

20......

20......

20......

20......

20......

20......

20......

MAY 14

20......

20......

20......

20......

20......

20......

20......

20......

20......

20......

20......

20......

20......

20......

20......

20......

20......

20......

20......

20......

MAY 18

20......

20......

20......

20......

20......

MAY 19

20......

20......

20......

20......

20......

20......

20......

20......

20......

20......

20......

20......

20......

20......

20......

MAY 22

20......

20......

20......

20......

20......

MAY 23

20......

20......

20......

20......

20......

MAY 24

20......

20......

20......

20......

20......

MAY 25

20......

20......

20......

20......

20......

MAY 26

20......

20......

20......

20......

20......

20......

20......

20......

20......

20......

MAY 28

20......

20......

20......

20......

20......

MAY 29

20......

20......

20......

20......

20......

MAY 30

20......

20......

20......

20......

20......

20......

20......

20......

20......

20......

JUNE 1

20......

20......

20......

20......

20......

JUNE 2

20......

20......

20......

20......

20......

JUNE 3

20......

20......

20......

20......

20......

JUNE 4

20......

20......

20......

20......

20......

JUNE 5

20......

20......

20......

20......

20......

20......

20......

20......

20......

20......

JUNE 7

20......

20......

20......

20......

20......

JUNE 8

20......

20......

20......

20......

20......

JUNE 9

20......

20......

20......

20......

20......

JUNE 10

20......

20......

20......

20......

20......

JUNE 11

20......

20......

20......

20......

20......

20......

20......

20......

20......

20......

JUNE 13

20......

20......

20......

20......

20......

JUNE 14

20......

20......

20......

20......

20......

JUNE 15

20......

20......

20......

20......

20......

20......

20......

20......

20......

20......

JUNE 17

20......

20......

20......

20......

20......

JUNE 18

20......

20......

20......

20......

20......

JUNE 19

20......

20......

20......

20......

20......

JUNE 20

20......

20......

20......

20......

20......

JUNE 21

20......

20......

20......

20......

20......

JUNE 22

20......

20......

20......

20......

20......

JUNE 23

20......

20......

20......

20......

20......

JUNE 24

20......

20......

20......

20......

20......

JUNE 25

20......

20......

20......

20......

20......

20......

20......

20......

20......

20......

JUNE 27

20......

20......

20......

20......

20......

JUNE 28

20......

20......

20......

20......

20......

JUNE 29

20......

20......

20......

20......

20......

JUNE 30

20......

20......

20......

20......

20......

JULY 1

20......

20......

20......

20......

20......

JULY 2

20......

20......

20......

20......

20......

JULY 3

20......

20......

20......

20......

20......

JULY 4

20......

20......

20......

20......

20......

JULY 5

20......

20......

20......

20......

20......

JULY 6

20......

20......

20......

20......

20......

JULY 7

20......

20......

20......

20......

20......

JULY 8

20......

20......

20......

20......

20......

JULY 9

20......

20......

20......

20......

20......

20.....

20.....

20.....

20.....

20.....

JULY 11

20......

20......

20......

20......

20......

JULY 12

20......

20......

20......

20......

20......

JULY 13

20......

20......

20......

20......

20......

JULY 14

20......

20......

20......

20......

20......

20......

20......

20......

20......

20......

JULY 16

20......

20......

20......

20......

20......

JULY 17

20......

20......

20......

20......

20......

20......

20......

20......

20......

20......

JULY 19

20......

20......

20......

20......

20......

20......

20......

20......

20......

20......

20......

20......

20......

20......

20......

20......

20......

20......

20......

20......

20......

20......

20......

20......

20......

20......

20......

20......

20......

20......

JULY 25

20......

20......

20......

20......

20......

20......

20......

20......

20......

20......

JULY 27

20......

20......

20......

20......

20......

JULY 28

20......

20......

20......

20......

20......

JULY 29

20......

20......

20......

20......

20......

JULY 30

20......

20......

20......

20......

20......

JULY 31

20......

20......

20......

20......

20......

AUGUST 1

20......

20......

20......

20......

20......

AUGUST 2

20......

20......

20......

20......

20......

AUGUST 3

20......

20......

20......

20......

20......

20......

20......

20......

20......

20......

20......

20......

20......

20......

20......

AUGUST 6

20......

20......

20......

20......

20......

20......

20......

20......

20......

20......

AUGUST 8

20......

20......

20......

20......

20......

AUGUST 9

20......

20......

20......

20......

20......

AUGUST 10

20......

20......

20......

20......

20......

AUGUST 11

20......

20......

20......

20......

20......

AUGUST 12

20......

20......

20......

20......

20......

AUGUST 13

20......

20......

20......

20......

20......

20......

20......

20......

20......

20......

AUGUST 15

20......

20......

20......

20......

20......

20......

20......

20......

20......

20......

AUGUST 17

20......

20......

20......

20......

20......

20......

20......

20......

20......

20......

20......

20......

20......

20......

20......

20......

20......

20......

20......

20......

20......

20......

20......

20......

20......

AUGUST 22

20......

20......

20......

20......

20......

20......

20......

20......

20......

20......

20_____

20_____

20_____

20_____

20_____

20......

20......

20......

20......

20......

AUGUST 26

20......

20......

20......

20......

20......

AUGUST 27

20......

20......

20......

20......

20......

AUGUST 28

20......

20......

20......

20......

20......

AUGUST 29

20......

20......

20......

20......

20......

20......

20......

20......

20......

20......

AUGUST 31

20......

20......

20......

20......

20......

SEPTEMBER 1

20......

20......

20......

20......

20......

20......

20......

20......

20......

20......

SEPTEMBER 3

20......

20......

20......

20......

20......

20......

20......

20......

20......

20......

20......

20......

20......

20......

20......

SEPTEMBER 6

20......

20......

20......

20......

20......

SEPTEMBER 7

20......

20......

20......

20......

20......

20......

20......

20......

20......

20......

20......

20......

20......

20......

20......

SEPTEMBER 10

20......

20......

20......

20......

20......

20......

20......

20......

20......

20......

SEPTEMBER 12

20......

20......

20......

20......

20......

SEPTEMBER 13

20......

20......

20......

20......

20......

20......

20......

20......

20......

20......

SEPTEMBER 15

20......

20......

20......

20......

20......

20......

20......

20......

20......

20......

SEPTEMBER 17

20......

20......

20......

20......

20......

SEPTEMBER 18

20......

20......

20......

20......

20......

SEPTEMBER 19

20......

20......

20......

20......

20......

20......

20......

20......

20......

20......

20......

20......

20......

20......

20......

SEPTEMBER 22

20......

20......

20......

20......

20......

SEPTEMBER 23

20......

20......

20......

20......

20......

20......

20......

20......

20......

20......

SEPTEMBER 25

20......

20......

20......

20......

20......

SEPTEMBER 26

20......

20......

20......

20......

20......

SEPTEMBER 27

20......

20......

20......

20......

20......

SEPTEMBER 28

20......

20......

20......

20......

20......

SEPTEMBER 29

20......

20......

20......

20......

20......

SEPTEMBER 30

20......

20......

20......

20......

20......

OCTOBER 1

20......

20......

20......

20......

20......

20......

20......

20......

20......

20......

OCTOBER 3

20......

20......

20......

20......

20......

OCTOBER 4

20......

20......

20......

20......

20......

OCTOBER 5

20......

20......

20......

20......

20......

OCTOBER 6

20......

20......

20......

20......

20......

20......

20......

20......

20......

20......

20......

20......

20......

20......

20......

OCTOBER 9

20......

20......

20......

20......

20......

OCTOBER 10

20......

20......

20......

20......

20......

OCTOBER 11

20......

20......

20......

20......

20......

OCTOBER 12

20......

20......

20......

20......

20......

OCTOBER 13

20......

20......

20......

20......

20......

OCTOBER 14

20......

20......

20......

20......

20......

OCTOBER 15

20......

20......

20......

20......

20......

OCTOBER 16

20......

20......

20......

20......

20......

20......

20......

20......

20......

20......

OCTOBER 18

20......

20......

20......

20......

20......

20......

20......

20......

20......

20......

20......

20......

20......

20......

20......

OCTOBER 21

20......

20......

20......

20......

20......

OCTOBER 22

20......

20......

20......

20......

20......

OCTOBER 23

20......

20......

20......

20......

20......

OCTOBER 24

20......

20......

20......

20......

20......

OCTOBER 25

20......

20......

20......

20......

20......

OCTOBER 26

20......

20......

20......

20......

20......

OCTOBER 27

20......

20......

20......

20......

20......

20......

20......

20......

20......

20......

OCTOBER 29

20......

20......

20......

20......

20......

OCTOBER 30

20......

20......

20......

20......

20......

OCTOBER 31

20......

20......

20......

20......

20......

20......

20......

20......

20......

20......

20......

20......

20......

20......

20......

20......

20......

20......

20......

20......

20......

20......

20......

20......

20......

NOVEMBER 5

20......

20......

20......

20......

20......

20......

20......

20......

20......

20......

20......

20......

20......

20......

20......

20......

20......

20......

20......

20......

NOVEMBER 9

20......

20......

20......

20......

20......

NOVEMBER 10

20......

20......

20......

20......

20......

NOVEMBER 11

20......

20......

20......

20......

20......

NOVEMBER 12

20......

20......

20......

20......

20......

20......

20......

20......

20......

20......

20......

20......

20......

20......

20......

NOVEMBER 15

20......

20......

20......

20......

20......

20......

20......

20......

20......

20......

20......

20......

20......

20......

20......

NOVEMBER 18

20......

20......

20......

20......

20......

20......

20......

20......

20......

20......

20.....

20.....

20.....

20.....

20.....

20......

20......

20......

20......

20......

NOVEMBER 22

20......

20......

20......

20......

20......

20......

20......

20......

20......

20......

NOVEMBER 24

20......

20......

20......

20......

20......

NOVEMBER 25

20......

20......

20......

20......

20......

20......

20......

20......

20......

20......

NOVEMBER 27

20......

20......

20......

20......

20......

NOVEMBER 28

20......

20......

20......

20......

20......

NOVEMBER 29

20......

20......

20......

20......

20......

NOVEMBER 30

20......

20......

20......

20......

20......

DECEMBER 1

20......

20......

20......

20......

20......

DECEMBER 2

20......

20......

20......

20......

20......

DECEMBER 3

20......

20......

20......

20......

20......

DECEMBER 4

20......

20......

20......

20......

20......

DECEMBER 5

20......

20......

20......

20......

20......

DECEMBER 6

20......

20......

20......

20......

20......

DECEMBER 7

20......

20......

20......

20......

20......

DECEMBER 8

20......

20......

20......

20......

20......

DECEMBER 9

20......

20......

20......

20......

20......

DECEMBER 10

20......

20......

20......

20......

20......

DECEMBER 11

20......

20......

20......

20......

20......

DECEMBER 12

20......

20......

20......

20......

20......

DECEMBER 13

20......

20......

20......

20......

20......

DECEMBER 14

20......

20......

20......

20......

20......

DECEMBER 15

20......

20......

20......

20......

20......

DECEMBER 16

20......

20......

20......

20......

20......

DECEMBER 17

20......

20......

20......

20......

20......

DECEMBER 18

20......

20......

20......

20......

20......

DECEMBER 19

20......

20......

20......

20......

20......

DECEMBER 20

20......

20......

20......

20......

20......

DECEMBER 21

20......

20......

20......

20......

20......

DECEMBER 22

20......

20......

20......

20......

20......

DECEMBER 23

20......

20......

20......

20......

20......

DECEMBER 24

20......

20......

20......

20......

20......

DECEMBER 25

20......

20......

20......

20......

20......

DECEMBER 26

20......

20......

20......

20......

20......

DECEMBER 27

20......

20......

20......

20......

20......

DECEMBER 28

20......

20......

20......

20......

20......

DECEMBER 29

20......

20......

20......

20......

20......

DECEMBER 30

20......

20......

20......

20......

20......

DECEMBER 31

20......

20......

20......

20......

20......

DATES TO REMEMBER